SAN DIEGO
CHARGERS

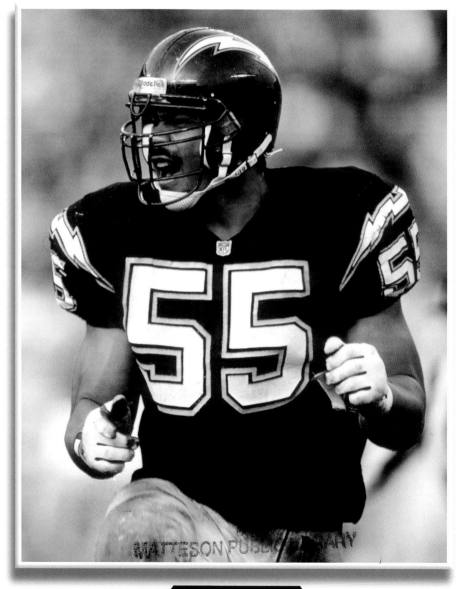

by Bernie Wilson

Published by ABDO Publishing Company, 8000 West 78th Street, Edina, Minnesota 55439. Copyright © 2011 by Abdo Consulting Group, Inc. International copyrights reserved in all countries. No part of this book may be reproduced in any form without written permission from the publisher. SportsZone™ is a trademark and logo of ABDO Publishing Company.

Printed in the United States of America,
North Mankato, Minnesota
062010
092010

Editor: Matt Tustison
Copy Editor: Nicholas Cafarelli
Interior Design and Production: Craig Hinton
Cover Design: Becky Daum

Photo Credits: Denis Poroy/AP Images, cover, 10, 34, 42 (top), 43 (bottom); NFL Photos/AP Images, title page, 13, 20, 23, 30, 43 (top), 44; George Widman/AP Images, 4; Gene J. Puskar/AP Images, 7; Eric Riseberg/AP Images, 8; AP Images, 14, 17, 18, 42 (middle, bottom); Lenny Ignelzi/AP Images, 24, 37; Bill Kostroun/AP Images, 26; David Stluka/AP Images, 29; Doug Mills/AP Images, 33, 43 (middle); Greg Trott/AP Images, 38; Paul Spinelli/AP Images, 41; Jeff Chiu/AP Images, 47

Library of Congress Cataloging-in-Publication Data
Wilson, Bernie.
 San Diego Chargers / Bernie Wilson.
   p. cm. — (Inside the NFL)
 ISBN 978-1-61714-026-6
 1. San Diego Chargers (Football team)—History—Juvenile literature. I. Title.
 GV956.S29W55 2011
 796.332'6409794985—dc22
                                2010017458

TABLE OF CONTENTS

CHAPTER 1

LIGHTNING STRIKES IN PITTSBURGH

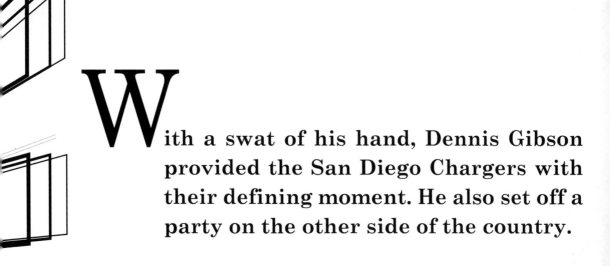

With a swat of his hand, Dennis Gibson provided the San Diego Chargers with their defining moment. He also set off a party on the other side of the country.

The Pittsburgh Steelers needed only 3 yards for the winning touchdown in the closing seconds of the American Football Conference (AFC) Championship Game on January 15, 1995.

It was fourth down. Quarterback Neil O'Donnell had been picking apart San Diego's defense as he moved Pittsburgh down its

THE CHARGERS' TONY MARTIN, *RIGHT*, AND MARK SEAY CELEBRATE MARTIN'S TOUCHDOWN CATCH IN THE AFC TITLE GAME IN JANUARY 1995.

home field. One more completion and the Steelers would be heading to Miami for the Super Bowl.

Pittsburgh had been to the Super Bowl four times, winning them all. San Diego was trying desperately to get there for the first time.

O'Donnell focused on running back Barry Foster. So did Gibson. The rugged linebacker swooped in front of Foster and knocked O'Donnell's pass to the turf. The Chargers jumped for joy as they ran off the field, their arms upraised.

Three Rivers Stadium went from the verge of mayhem to shocked silence on a rainy Sunday afternoon. Somehow, some way, the underdog Chargers had done it. They had held on for a 17–13 win. It sent them to the Super Bowl after all those years of coming up short.

"It's so funny. When I talk about my career, everybody wants to talk about 'The Play,'" Gibson said 15 years later. "I

> ## "It's so funny. When I talk about my career, everybody wants to talk about 'The Play.'"
>
> —Former Chargers linebacker Dennis Gibson, on his key defensive play late in the 1994 AFC Championship Game

THE CHARGERS' JUNIOR SEAU, *RIGHT*, AND THE STEELERS' JONATHAN HAYES EMBRACE AFTER THE AFC CHAMPIONSHIP GAME IN JANUARY 1995.

played nine seasons in the NFL [National Football League], but that's the one play that always gets brought up, and I guess that shows how special it was."

So special, in fact, that it is still talked about. During the

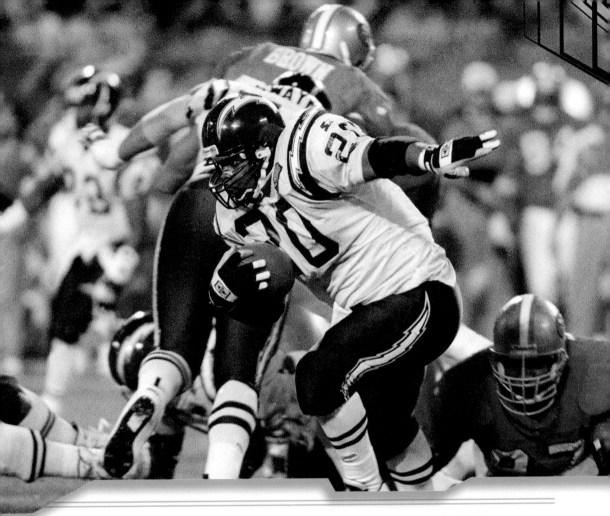

SAN DIEGO'S NATRONE MEANS TRIES TO BREAK AWAY AGAINST SAN FRANCISCO IN SUPER BOWL XXIX. THE CHARGERS LOST 49–26.

team's fiftieth anniversary celebration in 2009, fans picked it as the greatest single moment in Chargers history.

When the team returned to San Diego after the AFC title game, it was met by an estimated crowd of 70,000 at Jack Murphy Stadium that night.

The Chargers had been involved in plenty of big wins. But this one was the biggest.

A franchise that had been born 35 years earlier in Los Angeles was finally heading for the NFL's biggest stage.

The euphoria lasted just two weeks. The Chargers were routed 49–26 by the San Francisco 49ers in Super Bowl XXIX. Through 2009, that remained San Diego's only appearance in the NFL championship game.

Although the Chargers could not keep the momentum going after Gibson's big play, the team owned one championship from long ago.

The Chargers were a power from the opening days of the American Football League (AFL). The Chargers played in five of the first six AFL Championship Games, winning the title in 1963.

TOUCHDOWN TONY AND BIG ALFRED

Getting to the Super Bowl was not easy for the Chargers. It would have been impossible if not for wide receiver Tony Martin and H-back Alfred Pupunu.

Martin made a brilliant over-the-shoulder catch of a pass from Stan Humphries for a 43-yard touchdown. It gave San Diego the lead for good in the AFC title game against Pittsburgh, 17–13 with 5:13 to play.

In the third quarter, Pupunu caught a pass from Humphries and rumbled 43 yards down the middle of the field for a touchdown.

Pupunu's main job, usually, was to block in San Diego's running game. He was born in Tonga in the South Pacific. When he scored, he had a special ritual. He pretended to twist off the end of the football and drink kava juice as if from a coconut.

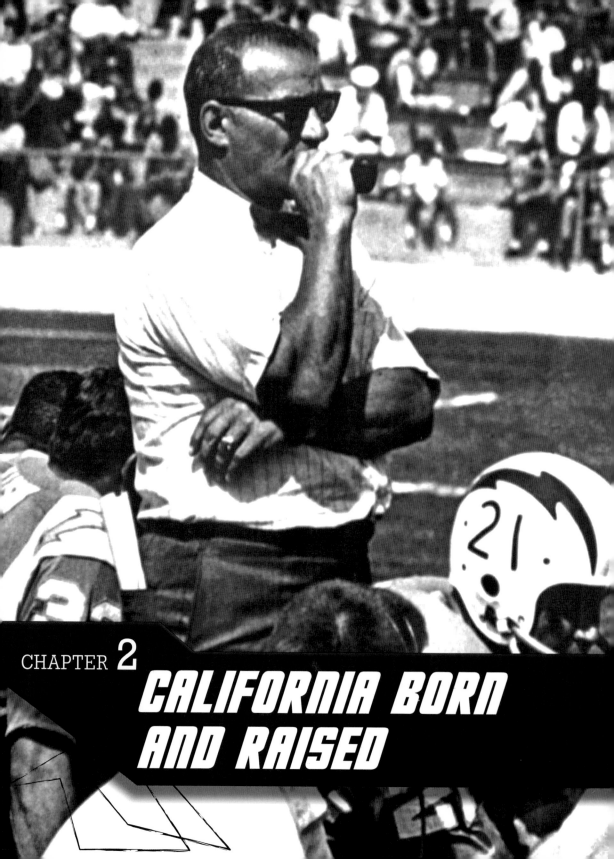

CHAPTER 2

CALIFORNIA BORN AND RAISED

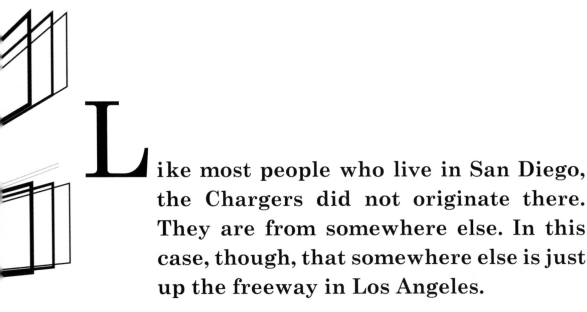

Like most people who live in San Diego, the Chargers did not originate there. They are from somewhere else. In this case, though, that somewhere else is just up the freeway in Los Angeles.

The Los Angeles Chargers were one of the AFL's eight original teams. The league began in 1960. It featured a colorful style of play before it merged with the NFL in 1970. The Chargers were owned by hotel heir Barron Hilton, grandfather of socialite and celebrity Paris Hilton.

The Chargers' name was chosen because "Charge" was what fans yelled at University of Southern California football games at the Los Angeles Memorial Coliseum. The Chargers' lightning bolt logo and team colors of blue and yellow date to the team's beginning.

SID GILLMAN, SHOWN SPORTING SHADES IN THE 1960s IN SUNNY SOUTHERN CALIFORNIA, WAS THE CHARGERS' FIRST COACH.

THE MURPH

One of the key figures in bringing the Chargers to San Diego was Jack Murphy. He was a columnist and sports editor at the *San Diego Union* newspaper.

Murphy would continue to have a big impact on the Chargers well beyond their move to San Diego in 1961. In the early 1960s, he began pushing for a new stadium. The idea was that the stadium could be the home to the Chargers and to the major league baseball team that Murphy was trying to attract. That new stadium opened in 1967. It was called San Diego Stadium.

In 1969, the expansion San Diego Padres baseball team began playing in the stadium. It was renamed Jack Murphy Stadium after his death in 1980. It became known simply as "The Murph." The name was changed to Qualcomm Stadium in 1997 to reflect that company's $18 million payment to the city to help with expanding the stadium.

The original team played football under coach Sid Gillman. The Chargers shared the Los Angeles Memorial Coliseum with the Rams of the NFL.

During the exhibition opener on August 6, 1960, at the Coliseum, Paul Lowe returned a kickoff 105 yards for a touchdown on the first play in team history. This helped the Chargers win 27–7 over the New York Titans. The Chargers were a hit in their first regular-season game as well. They rallied to beat the Dallas Texans 21–20.

Overall, it was a successful first season. The Chargers' leader was quarterback Jack Kemp. He would go on to become a congressman from New York and run for vice president of the United States in 1996. The Chargers finished with a record of 10–4 to win the Western Division. They advanced to the AFL

PAUL LOWE WAS A CHARGER FROM 1960 TO 1968. HE RETURNED A KICKOFF 105 YARDS FOR A SCORE IN THE TEAM'S FIRST EXHIBITION GAME.

Championship Game but lost 24–16 to the Houston Oilers.

Even as the Chargers were playing in that title game, Hilton had begun the process of exploring a move to San Diego. The Chargers seemed to be an afterthought in Los Angeles. They played in front of small crowds. San Diego was a quiet little Navy town where civic officials were hungry for major league sports.

That wish came true less than two months later. The AFL gave Hilton approval to move the team to San Diego. The capacity at Balboa Stadium was increased from 23,000 to 34,000.

A new chapter in the city's sports history was beginning.

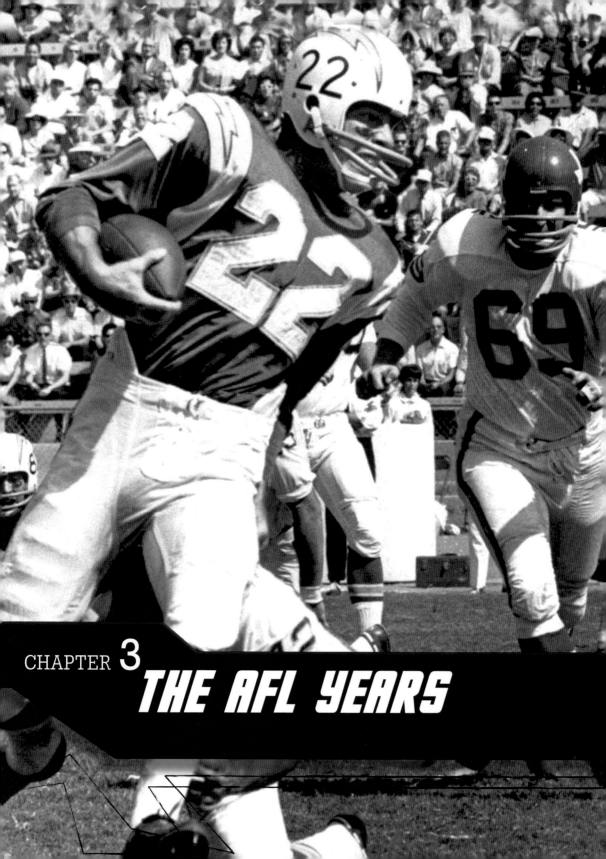

CHAPTER 3
THE AFL YEARS

Although the NFL was the established big brother, the AFL had a personality all its own. The Chargers fit right in with the new league.

The AFL had teams in Denver, Oakland, Houston, Dallas, Buffalo, Boston, and New York. The Dallas Texans eventually became the Kansas City Chiefs. Half of the original AFL now makes up the AFC West: San Diego, Kansas City, Oakland, and Denver. So rivalries that were brand new in 1960 are still going strong.

The Chargers did not have the growing pains so often

GILLMAN GETS IN

Sid Gillman was the Chargers' first coach and later their general manager. He was inducted into the Pro Football Hall of Fame in 1983. He was an innovator in the passing game and became the first coach to win division titles in both the NFL and the AFL. He had an overall record of 87–57–6 with the Chargers, including the playoffs.

THE CHARGERS' KEITH LINCOLN RUNS IN 1962. LINCOLN'S 349 TOTAL YARDS WOULD LEAD SAN DIEGO TO A BLOWOUT WIN IN THE 1963 AFL TITLE GAME.

associated with new teams. The AFL attracted some great players. The Chargers certainly had their share. Among them were quarterbacks Jack Kemp, Tobin Rote, and John Hadl, wide receiver Lance Alworth, and running backs Keith Lincoln and Paul Lowe.

Those players gave the Chargers an early identity and played high-scoring football. This thrilled the crowds that flocked to sun-splashed Balboa Stadium, located on the edge of downtown San Diego.

Lowe was fast, and Lincoln was tough. They could hit the hole and rip off huge chunks of yardage. Alworth was so fast and graceful that he was nicknamed "Bambi." It might not seem like the ideal nickname for a professional football player. But in this case, it fit. Kemp and then Rote and Hadl ran the show.

The Chargers had 10 or more wins in three of their first four seasons. They won the Western Division championship in 1960 and 1961.

But the Chargers just could not get past quarterback George Blanda and the Houston Oilers in the AFL Championship Game. The Oilers won the first AFL title by beating the Chargers 24–16 in Houston. The budding rivals met again for the AFL championship the next season. This time the game was played in San Diego. The result was the

LANCE ALWORTH, SHOWN IN 1967, WAS A STANDOUT WIDE RECEIVER FOR SAN DIEGO FROM 1962 TO 1970. HE IS IN THE PRO FOOTBALL HALL OF FAME.

same, though. Houston took the title with a 10–3 victory.

In 1963, it all came together for the Chargers. They won the Western Division with a record of 11–3 and got to host the AFL Championship Game at Balboa Stadium against the Boston Patriots. Lincoln responded with a remarkable game. He had

A MAN CALLED BAMBI

Lance Alworth remains one of the most popular Chargers ever, even 40 years after he caught his last pass with the team. He joined the team out of the University of Arkansas in 1962. He was nicknamed "Bambi" because of his graceful speed and ability to leap high to haul in passes. He was the epitome of the 1960s Chargers. The Chargers traded him to the Dallas Cowboys in 1971. In 1978, he became the first AFL player to be inducted into the Pro Football Hall of Fame.

VETERAN TOBIN ROTE, SHOWN IN 1964, WAS THE CHARGERS' STARTING
QUARTERBACK IN 1963, WHEN THEY ROLLED TO THE AFL CHAMPIONSHIP.

349 total yards and two touchdowns in leading the Chargers to a 51–10 victory.

Lincoln was almost unstoppable. He ran for 206 yards, including a 67-yard touchdown gallop that is still a highlight-reel favorite today. He caught seven passes for 123 yards and a touchdown. He even threw a pass for 20 yards.

The Chargers continued to play winning football through the rest of the 1960s. They made it to the 1964 and 1965 AFL title games but lost both times. They could not get back to the AFL championship contest the rest of the decade, despite having a winning record each season.

Through 2009, the 1963 AFL title remained the only major championship won by a San Diego team.

A new era would begin in 1970. That is when the Chargers, along with the rest of the AFL teams, joined the NFL.

1964, 1965 TITLE GAMES

After their 51–10 rout of the Boston Patriots in the 1963 AFL Championship Game, the Chargers made it back to the league's title contest each of the next two seasons. Both times, they faced a new rival and an old teammate: the Buffalo Bills and quarterback Jack Kemp. The Chargers, however, could not recapture the magic of 1963.

In the 1964 title contest, running back Keith Lincoln was forced out of the game with a broken rib. Wide receiver Lance Alworth already was missing because of an injury. Quarterback Tobin Rote threw two interceptions. Kemp sealed a 20–7 victory for host Buffalo with a 1-yard touchdown run.

The next year, the Chargers hosted the Bills in the title game. It was more of the same, though. John Hadl was intercepted twice, and the Chargers lost 23–0. Kemp threw a touchdown pass for Buffalo.

CHAPTER 4

AIR CORYELL TAKES OFF

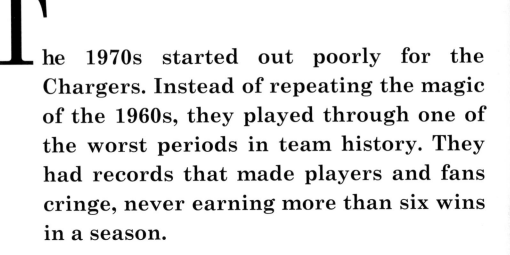

The 1970s started out poorly for the Chargers. Instead of repeating the magic of the 1960s, they played through one of the worst periods in team history. They had records that made players and fans cringe, never earning more than six wins in a season.

However, one big move that would shape their future had already been made. Several more important moves would come later in the decade.

In what would turn out to be one of the most significant draft picks in team history, the Chargers selected quarterback Dan Fouts from the University of Oregon in the third round of the 1973 NFL Draft. The Chargers also acquired star quarterback Johnny Unitas from the Baltimore Colts that year. He only played one season with the Chargers before he retired.

Fouts was a rugged, hard-nosed competitor who was easily recognized by his bushy beard.

THE CHARGERS' DAN FOUTS THREW THE BALL OFTEN, AND WITH GREAT SUCCESS, IN THE LATE 1970s AND EARLY 1980s UNDER COACH DON CORYELL.

He struggled along with the rest of the Chargers through the dismal years of the early- to mid-1970s. He was winless in six starts as a rookie. He then went 3–8 in his second season. That is how it went for the next few seasons as the Chargers struggled to find their identity.

That identity would begin to be formed almost immediately after San Diego hired Don Coryell as coach on September 25, 1978. The Chargers had started that season with a 1–3 record. That led coach Tommy Prothro to quit. San Diego fans were already familiar with Coryell. He had coached at San Diego State University from 1961 to 1972. The Chargers lost their first game under Coryell and three of their first four. But then things began to click. They finished 9–7 in 1978 for their first winning season since 1969.

It was the beginning of "Air Coryell." This would be the era in which the high-flying Chargers would redefine the passing game in the NFL. Coryell turned Fouts loose. He responded with three straight seasons in which he passed for more than 4,000 yards.

Fouts's favorite targets were not always wide receivers Charlie Joiner and Wes Chandler. In 1979, the Chargers made another innovation. They drafted tight end Kellen Winslow. He proved that tight ends do not always have to block. Winslow became

HALL OF FAMERS

There is a pretty good reason why the Air Coryell years were so good. Four players from those teams ended up being voted into the Pro Football Hall of Fame. Quarterback Dan Fouts, tight end Kellen Winslow, wide receiver Charlie Joiner, and defensive end Fred Dean all earned their Hall of Fame credentials during this era.

DON CORYELL COACHED THE CHARGERS FROM 1978 TO 1986. HE LED THEM TO THE PLAYOFFS FOUR TIMES. SAN DIEGO'S PASSING OFFENSE HAD MUCH SUCCESS UNDER HIM.

one of the premier pass catchers in the NFL. He led the team in receptions for four straight years, from 1980 to 1983. He was fast and strong. Opponents simply could not figure out a way to stop him.

The Chargers went 12–4 in 1979 and returned to the play-offs for the first time in 14 years. They suffered a disappointing 17–14 loss to the Houston Oilers in the divisional round. The Chargers went 11–5 and made the postseason again the next year. They earned some long-overdue revenge against the Buffalo Bills, beating them 20–14 in the divisional round.

CHARGERS TIGHT END KELLEN WINSLOW MAKES A CATCH AGAINST THE STEELERS IN 1980. WINSLOW WAS A BIG PART OF SAN DIEGO'S PASSING ATTACK DURING THE "AIR CORYELL" ERA.

That earned the Chargers a shot at the rival Oakland Raiders in the AFC Championship Game. With a trip to the Super Bowl at stake, the host Chargers fell behind by three touchdowns in the first half. They simply could not catch up. They lost 34–27.

"SAN DIEGO SUPER CHARGERS"

Perhaps one of the catchiest fight songs of all time originated during the Air Coryell years. It is a disco song titled "San Diego Super Chargers." It is played to this day at Qualcomm Stadium. It was recorded in a Los Angeles studio in 1979 by R&B vocalist James Gaylen and released under the name "Captain Q.B. & the Big Boys."

The next season, the Chargers would play in perhaps two of the most memorable playoff games in the history of pro football. The games were held in extreme conditions.

The Chargers beat the Dolphins 41–38 in overtime in tropical Miami. The game could only be described as an epic struggle. The next week, however, the Chargers were completely out of their element. They traveled to frozen Cincinnati and lost 27–7 to the Bengals in the AFC Championship Game. It was the coldest day in NFL history. The wind-chill factor was minus 59 at kickoff. It is no wonder that the Chargers' offense froze up.

The Chargers never did make it to the Super Bowl under Coryell. That fact often is lost in the pure excitement that those years provided.

INSTANT CLASSIC

San Diego's 41–38 overtime victory in the playoffs at Miami on January 2, 1982, remains one of the greatest games in NFL history, many people believe.

The Chargers jumped to a 24–0 lead in the first quarter. They then fell behind, and then they tied the score on Dan Fouts's 9-yard touchdown pass to James Brooks with 58 seconds left in regulation. Finally, after 13:52 had elapsed in the 15-minute overtime, Rolf Benirschke kicked a winning 27-yard field goal.

One of the lasting images of the Air Coryell era was that of exhausted tight end Kellen Winslow being helped off the field by two teammates, with a towel over his head. Despite cramping up in the heat and humidity, he caught 13 passes for 166 yards and one touchdown. He also blocked a potential game-winning field goal.

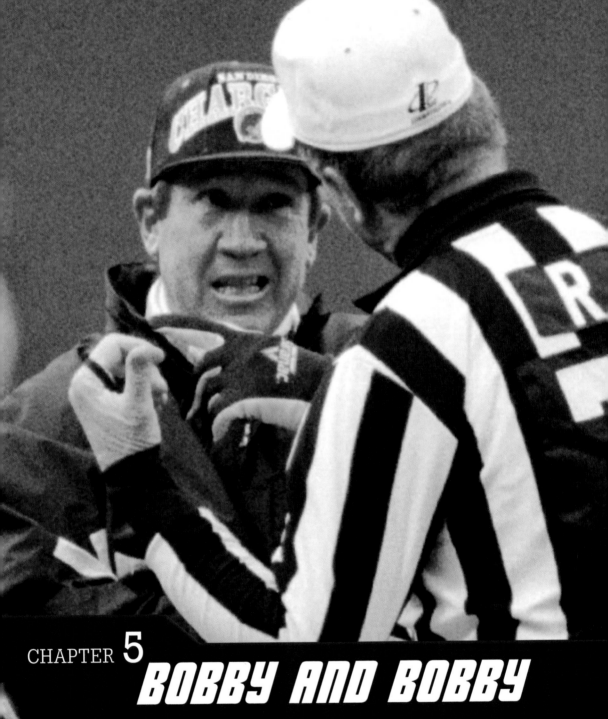

CHAPTER 5

BOBBY AND BOBBY

The Chargers had a frustrating habit of going into long slumps. It happened again in the 1980s. The Chargers returned to the playoffs in 1982. But then Air Coryell started coming back to earth. The playoff berths dried up. The Air Coryell era officially ended on October 29, 1986.

That is when Don Coryell resigned as coach after a 1–7 start. It was a sad day in San Diego's sports history. Quarterback Dan Fouts then retired after the 1987 season. He finally could not handle any more of the poundings he was absorbing.

Head coaches and starting quarterbacks would come and go. Losing seasons piled up. Then, just as earlier in team history, it took just one hire to start the process of turning the team around. On January 3, 1990, the Chargers hired Bobby Beathard as general manager. He had spent the previous decade building the Washington Redskins into perennial champions. The

SAN DIEGO COACH BOBBY ROSS TALKS WITH REFEREE RON BLUM IN 1995. ROSS WAS THE CHARGERS' COACH FROM 1992 TO 1996. HE LED THEM TO THE PLAYOFFS THREE TIMES.

Redskins played in three Super Bowls and won two during the 1980s.

Beathard's first draft pick was a beauty. He selected linebacker Junior Seau from the University of Southern California with the fifth pick overall in the 1990 NFL Draft. Seau had grown up in Oceanside, a suburb of San Diego. He brought an instant spark to the defense with his high-energy play. Seau knew only one speed: full speed ahead. He played the same way whether it was in practice or on Sundays.

The turnaround under Beathard took time. The Chargers were 6–10 and 4–12 in his first two seasons in charge. That led him to make another outstanding decision. He reached into the college ranks and hired coach Bobby Ross from Georgia Tech before the 1992 season. He also traded with the Redskins for quarterback Stan Humphries during training camp. That move turned out to be very beneficial because starting quarterback John Friesz injured a knee during an exhibition game. Bob Gagliano started the season

AS GENERAL MANAGER, BOBBY BEATHARD, SHOWN IN 1997, HELPED PUT TOGETHER THE COACHING STAFFS AND ROSTERS FOR SOME SUCCESSFUL CHARGERS TEAMS IN THE 1990s.

MARION BUTTS MOVES DOWN THE FIELD ON A 54-YARD TOUCHDOWN RUN
DURING SAN DIEGO'S 17–0 PLAYOFF WIN OVER KANSAS CITY IN JANUARY 1993.

opener. But Humphries had won the job by the second game.

The Ross-Humphries era did not get off to a great start. The Chargers lost their first four games. They finished 11–5, however, and won the AFC West. They became the first team in NFL history to lose their first four games and still make the

DOUBLE TRAGEDY

The Chargers were struck by tragedy twice in an 11-month period in the mid-1990s. On June 19, 1995, linebacker David Griggs was killed in a car accident in Davie, Florida, near his home. His death came one week after the team received its AFC championship rings. On May 11, 1996, running back Rodney Culver and his wife were killed in the crash of ValuJet Flight 592 in the Florida Everglades.

playoffs. They returned to the postseason after a nine-year absence and defeated the division rival Kansas City Chiefs 17–0.

The atmosphere was exciting that afternoon in San Diego despite rain. That was especially the case after big running back Marion Butts broke loose on a 54-yard touchdown run up the middle for the game's first score in the third quarter.

To celebrate the victory, the team resurrected its disco-era song, "San Diego Super Chargers." The Bolts were back.

The Chargers went from one shutout to another. The next week, they lost 31–0 in the rain at Miami. It was a disappointing end to a remarkable season. But Chargers fans embraced the feeling of a winning record and a return to the playoffs.

STAN THE MAN

Stan Humphries might not have been one of the most glamorous quarterbacks in the NFL in the 1990s. But he probably was one of the toughest. He played college ball at Northeast Louisiana University before going to the Washington Redskins. He won a Super Bowl ring after the 1991 season as the Redskins' third-string quarterback. He was always a favorite of Bobby Beathard's. That is why he ended up with the Chargers. He was strong enough to throw the deep pass and occasionally block for running backs.

Two years later, the Chargers put it all together. They finished 11–5, won the AFC West title, and earned a first-round bye. They rallied to beat visiting Miami 22–21 in their playoff opener. They then stunned the Steelers 17–13 in Pittsburgh to advance to the Super Bowl for the first time. It was an all-California final: the Chargers against the San Francisco 49ers.

San Diego had Super Bowl fever. While few people outside the city thought the Chargers

SUPER ROUT

Super Bowl XXIX on January 29, 1995, at Joe Robbie Stadium in Miami quickly turned into a nightmare for the Chargers and their fans.

San Diego was a big underdog to the San Francisco 49ers, and the reason quickly became evident. Less than five minutes into the game, the 49ers had taken a 14-0 lead on touchdown passes from Steve Young to Jerry Rice and Ricky Watters.

San Diego marched down the field, and running back Natrone Means leaped over a pile of players for a 1-yard touchdown that cut the deficit to 14-7. But San Francisco responded with another touchdown. The rout was on. The Chargers were stunned.

The final score of 49-26 turned out to be just as bad as some experts had predicted it would be.

could win, the team's fans were confident. Unfortunately for the Chargers, they were overwhelmed in one of the biggest blowouts in Super Bowl history. They allowed a Super Bowl-record six touchdown passes by 49ers quarterback Steve Young and were routed 49–26. Seau had a vacant stare on his face along the sideline late in the game.

Ross silently fumed in the locker room afterward as he waited to be interviewed on TV. Players who had allowed the 49ers to score almost at will sat at their lockers, their heads in their hands. It was not the way the team and its fans ever thought it would end.

Despite the blowout, the Chargers were welcomed back the next day with a parade through downtown San Diego. The shock was still fresh. But

CHARGERS QUARTERBACK STAN HUMPHRIES REACTS DURING SAN DIEGO'S 49–26 LOSS TO SAN FRANCISCO IN SUPER BOWL XXIX ON JANUARY 29, 1995.

fans wanted to celebrate a breakthrough season.

Behind the scenes, the relationship between Beathard and Ross was falling apart. Beathard had been taking chances with his draft picks and wanted Ross to use some of the younger players more. The coach held his ground. He stuck with the players he thought gave the team the best chance to win. The rift widened. On January 3, 1997, Ross resigned and his staff was fired.

Another era in the team's up-and-down history had ended.

CHAPTER 6
TOMLINSON'S TIME

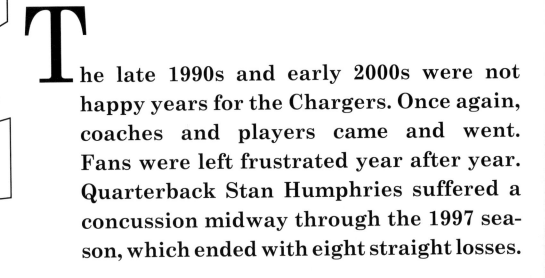

The late 1990s and early 2000s were not happy years for the Chargers. Once again, coaches and players came and went. Fans were left frustrated year after year. Quarterback Stan Humphries suffered a concussion midway through the 1997 season, which ended with eight straight losses.

Unable to shake the scary effects of the latest of a handful of concussions, Humphries tearfully announced his retirement on February 27, 1998. He walked away with the distinction of being the only quarterback to get the Chargers to the Super Bowl.

THEY SAID IT

"I was very fortunate because it was a time where he allowed me to kind of prove what I could do in this league. He put the ball in my belly. That's all I could ask from a coach. He believed in me, and I appreciate that."
—LaDainian Tomlinson, on the influence coach Marty Schottenheimer had on him early in his career

THE CHARGERS' LADAINIAN TOMLINSON HAD A LOT TO SMILE ABOUT IN 2006. HE RAN FOR 1,815 YARDS AND SET AN NFL RECORD WITH 31 TOUCHDOWNS.

Needing a quarterback, San Diego traded up one spot to number two in the 1998 NFL Draft. After the Indianapolis Colts selected quarterback Peyton Manning, the Chargers took quarterback Ryan Leaf.

At the time, it was the logical thing to do. But it turned out to be a mistake that set the team back for years. Leaf showed promise by winning his first two starts. But he began having meltdowns on and off the field. Leaf was finally released after the 2000 season. The Chargers hit an all-time low that season by going 1–15.

That embarrassing finish led owner Alex Spanos to hire tough-guy general manager John Butler. Butler was not afraid to take chances. His biggest was to trade the number one pick overall in the 2001 NFL Draft to the Atlanta Falcons for a package

ANTONIO GATES

Few players have as interesting a story and as quick a rise in the NFL as Chargers tight end Antonio Gates. Gates first rose to prominence as a college basketball player. He helped lead Kent State University within one win of the Final Four in 2002. Knowing that he probably had a better chance of playing pro football than going to the National Basketball Association, he signed with the Chargers as a rookie free agent in 2003. Opposing defenses almost immediately found him hard to cover because of his size and leaping ability. He was the team's leading receiver every season from 2004 to 2009. Through 2009, he had been selected to the Pro Bowl six times and to the All-Pro team three times.

of draft picks and players. With the number five pick, the Chargers selected Texas Christian University star LaDainian Tomlinson. It is hard to believe now, but there were some Chargers fans who were not happy. They wanted quarterback Michael Vick, whom Atlanta selected. The player San Diego got, however, turned out to be one of the top running backs in NFL

LADAINIAN TOMLINSON WAS A ROOKIE STAR IN 2001. HE RAN FOR 1,236 YARDS. "L. T." WOULD ALSO RUSH FOR 1,000 YARDS IN EACH OF THE NEXT SEVEN SEASONS.

history. He would become known simply by his initials: L. T.

Tomlinson began establishing himself as a star from his first game, when he gained 113 yards and scored two touchdowns. The rebuilding process took a few years under coach Marty Schottenheimer. By 2004, though, the Chargers had returned to the playoffs.

Two years later, Tomlinson had one of the most remarkable seasons in league history. He scored 31 touchdowns and 186 points, both NFL records. On a memorable afternoon at Qualcomm Stadium, he scored three touchdowns against the Denver Broncos to become the touchdown record holder. After his third touchdown run of the day, his massive offensive linemen

lifted him onto their shoulders and carried him to the sideline. L. T. held the ball in one hand and raised the index finger of his other hand toward the crowd.

Tomlinson was the runaway pick as the NFL's Most Valuable Player in 2006. He was the first Chargers player to receive the league's ultimate individual honor. Although he was clearly the star, the Chargers were slowly but surely building one of the most talented teams in the NFL. Among the other stars were quarterback Philip Rivers, tight end Antonio Gates, wide receiver Vincent Jackson, and outside linebacker Shawne Merriman.

QUARTERBACK PHILIP RIVERS WAS PART OF A TALENTED GROUP OF SAN DIEGO PLAYERS IN THE 2000s. THE TEAM DID NOT ALWAYS SUCCEED IN THE PLAYOFFS, HOWEVER.

THE BIG TRADE

A few days before the 2004 NFL Draft, Archie Manning, a former quarterback in the league, asked the Chargers not to pick his son Eli with the number one selection.

The Chargers were coming off a 4–12 season. The Manning family apparently felt it was not a good situation for Eli, the younger brother of Colts star quarterback Peyton Manning.

Chargers general manager A. J. Smith picked Manning anyway. Smith then made one of the biggest trades in team history. He sent Manning to the New York Giants for the rights to quarterback Philip Rivers, a third-round choice that the Chargers used to select kicker Nate Kaeding, a 2005 first-round pick that the team used to select outside linebacker Shawne Merriman, and a 2005 fifth-round pick that San Diego traded to Tampa Bay for offensive tackle Roman Oben.

With that talented roster, the Chargers enjoyed a lot of regular-season success. The team won five AFC West titles from 2004 to 2009.

The playoffs were a different story, however. The furthest San Diego could advance during that time was the AFC Championship Game after the 2007 season. Under first-year coach Norv Turner, the visiting Chargers lost 21–12 to the New England Patriots. The Patriots improved to 18–0 that season, counting playoff games, with that win. But New England would lose 17–14 to the New York Giants in the Super Bowl.

During this period, Tomlinson was the heart and soul of the Chargers. His value to San Diego extended beyond the football field. He was active in many charitable activities, including distributing thousands of Thanksgiving dinners to the needy every year. He was quiet and humble. He conducted himself with class. He had become one of the city's most beloved athletes, right up there with former Chargers quarterback Dan Fouts and former San Diego Padres baseball star Tony Gwynn.

Everyone knew who No. 21 was. Injuries and age took their toll on Tomlinson, though. The Chargers released him several weeks after their 2009 season ended with a playoff loss to the

L. T.'S RECORDS

LaDainian Tomlinson owns or shares 28 team records. During his nine seasons in San Diego, Tomlinson won two NFL rushing titles (2006 and 2007) and set NFL single-season records for touchdowns (31 in 2006) and rushing touchdowns (28 in 2006). He also set the NFL mark for most consecutive games with a rushing touchdown (18, 2004–2005). He left the Chargers after the 2009 season with 12,490 rushing yards. That was the eighth-best total in NFL history at that point.

TIGHT END ANTONIO GATES BREAKS AWAY FROM COLTS DEFENDERS IN THE CHARGERS' 23–17 OVERTIME WILD-CARD PLAYOFF WIN ON JANUARY 3, 2009.

New York Jets. Tomlinson bid a tearful farewell to the fans who had cheered him so many years. He signed a two-year contract with the Jets in March 2010.

Once again a star was leaving. As with previous eras, though, Chargers fans know there will be other players who will write their own successful chapters in the team's long, colorful history.

TIMELINE

1960	The Chargers play the first regular-season game in franchise history, beating the visiting Dallas Texans 21–20 on September 10.
1961	The Chargers receive permission from the AFL on February 10 to move to San Diego from Los Angeles.
1961	The Chargers play their first regular-season game in San Diego, beating the Oakland Raiders 44–0 on September 17.
1964	Keith Lincoln accounts for 349 yards of total offense as the host Chargers win the AFL Championship Game, 51–10 against the Boston Patriots on January 5.
1967	San Diego Stadium is dedicated on August 20 before an exhibition loss to the Detroit Lions, the Chargers' first game against an NFL team.
1973	The Chargers obtain future Hall of Fame quarterback Johnny Unitas from the Baltimore Colts on January 22.
1978	On January 23, former Chargers wide receiver Lance Alworth becomes the first player from the AFL to be elected to the Pro Football Hall of Fame.
1980	San Diego Mayor Pete Wilson announces on December 22 that San Diego Stadium will be renamed San Diego Jack Murphy Stadium in honor of the late sports editor of the *San Diego Union*.

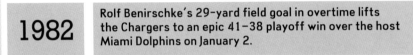

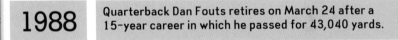

1982	Rolf Benirschke's 29-yard field goal in overtime lifts the Chargers to an epic 41–38 playoff win over the host Miami Dolphins on January 2.
1988	Quarterback Dan Fouts retires on March 24 after a 15-year career in which he passed for 43,040 yards.
1990	Bobby Beathard is hired as general manager on January 3.
1995	The Chargers play in their only Super Bowl, losing 49–26 on January 29 to the San Francisco 49ers at Joe Robbie Stadium in Miami.
2001	On April 21, the Chargers select running back LaDainian Tomlinson and quarterback Drew Brees with their first two picks of the NFL Draft.
2006	Tomlinson scores three touchdowns on December 10 against the visiting Denver Broncos to break Shaun Alexander's NFL single-season record of 28. Tomlinson would extend the record to 31.
2007	Tomlinson is named the NFL's Most Valuable Player on January 4. He becomes the first player in team history to win the honor.
2010	The Chargers release Tomlinson on February 22. He would sign with the New York Jets the next month.

QUICK STATS

FRANCHISE HISTORY

Los Angeles Chargers (1960)
San Diego Chargers (1961–)

SUPER BOWLS

1994 (XXIX)

AFL CHAMPIONSHIP GAMES
(1960–69; wins in bold)

1960, 1961, **1963**, 1964, 1965

AFC CHAMPIONSHIP GAMES
(since 1970 AFL-NFL merger)

1980, 1981, 1994, 2007

DIVISION CHAMPIONSHIPS
(since 1970 AFL-NFL merger)

1979, 1980, 1981, 1992, 1994, 2004,
2006, 2007, 2008, 2009

KEY PLAYERS
(position, seasons with team)

Lance Alworth (WR, 1962–70)
Fred Dean (DE, 1975–81)
Dan Fouts (QB, 1973–87)
Antonio Gates (TE, 2003–)
Charlie Joiner (WR, 1976–86)
Keith Lincoln (RB; 1961–66, 1968)
Ron Mix (OT, 1960–69)
Philip Rivers (QB, 2004–)
Junior Seau (LB, 1990–2002)
LaDainian Tomlinson (RB, 2001–09)
Kellen Winslow (TE, 1979–87)

KEY COACHES

Don Coryell (1978–86):
    69–56–0; 3–4 (playoffs)
Sid Gillman (1960–69, 1971):
    86–53–6; 1–4 (playoffs)
Bobby Ross (1992–96):
    47–33–0; 3–3 (playoffs)

HOME FIELDS

Qualcomm Stadium (1967–)
    Also known as Jack Murphy
    Stadium (1981–97) and San Diego
    Stadium (1967–80)
Balboa Stadium (1961–66)
Los Angeles Memorial Coliseum
    (1960)

* All statistics through 2009 season

QUOTES AND ANECDOTES

"After 15 years, this body has taken about as many hits as it can."
—Quarterback Dan Fouts, in announcing his retirement on March 24, 1988

"They thought this was only a tourist attraction. They know about Shamu. Now the world is going to know, not about Junior Seau, not about Natrone Means, not about Stan Humphries, not about Leslie O'Neal, but about the San Diego Chargers."
—Linebacker Junior Seau, to the estimated 70,000 fans who packed Jack Murphy Stadium to welcome home the Chargers after they upset the Pittsburgh Steelers in the AFC Championship Game on January 15, 1995

"For them to do the things they did, it's embarrassing for us. You feel like those guys are your peers and that something like this isn't supposed to happen."
—Cornerback Darrien Gordon, after the Chargers were routed 49–26 by the San Francisco 49ers in the Super Bowl on January 29, 1995

"This gets us out of the history books."
—Coach Mike Riley, after the Chargers beat the Kansas City Chiefs 17–16 on November 26, 2000, to improve to 1–11 and avoid potentially going 0–16. San Diego finished 1–15 that season.

GLOSSARY

concussion

An injury to the brain usually sustained when a football player's head is slammed to the turf.

exhibition game

A game, typically played before the official start of the season, that does not factor into the standings.

franchise

An entire sports organization, including the players, coaches, and staff.

general manager

The executive who is in charge of the team's overall operation. He or she hires and fires coaches, drafts college players, and signs free agents.

H-back

A player whose position is a combination of tight end and fullback. He usually blocks for the tailback but can also catch passes.

legendary

Well known and admired over a long period.

NFL Draft

The process by which teams select college players each spring. Teams pick based on the record the previous season, with teams with the worst records picking first.

retire

To officially end one's career.

rival

An opponent that brings out great emotion in a team and its players.

rookie

A first-year professional athlete.

Super Bowl

The NFL championship game. Because it is played in the calendar year following the regular season, it is designated with Roman numerals.

tight end

The player who lines up to the outside of the offensive tackle. He often blocks for the running back but can also catch passes.

FOR MORE INFORMATION

Further Reading

Brooks, Sid, with Geri Brooks. *Sid Brooks' Tales from the San Diego Chargers Locker Room*. Champaign, IL: Sports Publishing LLC, 2006.

Tobias, Todd. *Bombs Away! Air Coryell and the San Diego Chargers*. n.p.: Bandana Publishers, 2006.

Tomlinson, Loreane, Ginger Kolbaba, and Patti M. Britton. *LT & Me*. Carol Stream, IL: Tyndale House Publishers, 2009.

Web Links

To learn more about the San Diego Chargers, visit ABDO Publishing Company online at **www.abdopublishing.com.** Web sites about the Chargers are featured on our Book Links page. These links are routinely monitored and updated to provide the most current information available.

Places to Visit

Pro Football Hall of Fame
2121 George Halas Drive Northwest
Canton, OH 44708
330-456-8207
www.profootballhof.com
This hall of fame and museum highlights the greatest players and moments in the history of the National Football League. As of 2010, 11 people affiliated with the Chargers were enshrined, including Lance Alworth, Dan Fouts, Sid Gillman, and Kellen Winslow.

Qualcomm Stadium
9449 Friars Road
San Diego, CA 92108
619-280-2121
www.sandiego.gov/qualcomm
This is where the Chargers play all their home games.

San Diego Hall of Champions
2131 Pan American Plaza
San Diego, CA 92101
619-234-2544
www.sdhoc.com
The San Diego Hall of Champions, located in Balboa Park, is a multisport museum. The Hall of Champions recognizes San Diego's athletic accomplishments, including those of the Chargers.

INDEX

About the Author

Bernie Wilson has worked for The Associated Press since 1984, based in Spokane, Washington, Los Angeles, California, and San Diego, California. He has covered the San Diego Chargers since 1991, including their Super Bowl appearance after the 1994 season.